The eternal
God is
your
dwelling

place, and underneath
are the everlasting arms.
Deuteronomy 33:27

For God so loved the world, that he gave his only Son, that whoever believes in him should not perish

but have eternal life. John 3:16

Whoever believes in the Son has eternal life; whoever does not obey the Son shall not see life. John 3:36

Do not labour for the food that perishes, but for the food that endures to eternal life, which the Son of Man will give to you. John 6:27

Everyone who looks on the Son and believes in him should have eternal life. John 6:40

I give them eternal life, and they will never perish, and no one will snatch them out of my hand. John 10:28

This is eternal life, that they know you the only true God, and Jesus Christ whom you have sent. John 17:3

God's eternal power and divine nature, have been clearly perceived, ever since the creation of

the world, in the things that have been made. So they are without excuse. Romans 1:20

The wages of sin is death, but the free gift of God is eternal life in Christ Jesus our Lord. Romans 6:23

Fight the good fight of the faith. Take hold of the eternal life to which you were called. 1 Timothy 6:12

After you have suffered a little while, the God of all grace, who has called you to his eternal glory in

Christ, will himself restore, confirm, strengthen, and establish you.

1 Peter 5:10

Keep yourselves in the love of God, waiting for the mercy of our Lord Jesus Christ that leads to eternal life. Jude 1:21

And this is the promise that he made to us – eternal life. 1 John 2:25

What does the word eternal mean? It means never-ending or someone or something that has always existed. God is eternal. Humans are not like God. God is holy and perfect. We are sinners. God is the only one who has never had a beginning and will never have an end. Our bodies and our souls have a beginning when we are born and our bodies have an end when we die. However, our souls are eternal because they are one part of us that will not end.

Your soul is the part of you that worships God and trusts in Jesus. If your soul doesn't trust in Jesus then you will not go to heaven or have eternal life when you die. If your soul trusts in Jesus to take away the guilt of your sin and wrong doing then you will be given an eternal life by God. You will go to heaven to be with God when you die. What will that be like? You will spend forever with God the Father, God the Son and God the Holy Spirit. You will know them and love them and you will never sin again. Eternal life is glorious just as God is glorious.